A GOOD
FIRST STEP

Publisher's Cataloging in Publication
(Prepared by quality books Inc.)

Hamel, Richard A.
   A good first step: a first step workbook for twelve step
programs / Richard A Hamel. -- 2nd ed.
   p. cm.
   ISBN 0-89638-318-0

   1. Alcoholics--Rehabilitation. 2. Drug addicts--Rehabilitation.
   3. Twelve-step programs. I. Title.

HV5279.H35 1993   362.29'286
                          QBI93-933

Cover design by Jeremy Gale

**Inquiries, orders, and catalog requests should be addressed to
CompCare Publishers
Call 559-4800 or toll free 800-328-3330**

12	13	14	15
	93	94	95

Foreword

Of all Twelve Steps, which is the most important? It has to be that golden Number One. Why do anything about a problem when you believe no problem exists? Everything begins here. A good First Step makes or breaks the recovery process.

Most of us in the chemical dependency field are aware of a large segment of the alcoholic and drug-dependent populace who have spent years voicing the fact that they are indeed alcoholic, or dependent on drugs, but who have never come close to completing the First Step. Taking the First Step is very serious business indeed. It is the solid foundation on which quality sobriety is constructed. A weak foundation equals a shaky sobriety. The First Step demands profound soul-searching and exhaustive mental effort. The problem is that most do not know how to go about it.

This workbook has taken the guesswork out of what a thorough First Step entails. If an alcoholic takes the time, honestly follows these directions, and expends the necessary energy, he or she will be rewarded with the knowledge that few stones were left unturned. The alcoholic is forced to invade sacrosanct mental and emotional preserves that many people conveniently ignore. Using this First Step makes it difficult to hide behind phony subterfuge.

This is an excellent approach to a deeper, more thorough First Step. A superficial First Step simply doesn't work as a basis for recovery. If the recovering person follows this text thoughtfully, he or she cannot help but face head-on the reality of the price exacted by the disease of alcoholism/chemical dependency. A good First Step is indeed the first — and most valuable — step toward healthy sobriety.

Richard L. Reilly, D.O., Medical Director
Westcenter Alcoholism Unit
Tucson (Arizona) General Hospital

During the past few years an increasing number of chemical dependency treatment centers across the country and in Canada have made use of a written First Step as an important tool of therapy.

The First Step in written form is an important aid for the recovering person in coming to terms with the full import of what alcoholism really means. It is an instrument which helps us more fully understand in everyday terms the concepts of "powerlessness" and "unmanageability." These are powerful concepts indeed.

This First Step workbook is the most comprehensive First Step guide that I have found in the many years I have been involved in the field of substance abuse treatment. While particularly helpful to an individual in a professional treatment setting, it can be used effectively by any person who wishes to examine honestly the extent of a possible problem with mood-modifying substances, regardless of the setting.

James Guderjohn, M.S., Program Director
Summit Place Treatment Center
Mesa (Arizona) General Hospital

Author's introduction

This workbook is a tool to assist us in taking the first step away from alcoholism and other drug dependencies. It is not intended to be an explanation of the First Step of the Alcoholics Anonymous Program. AA's classic "Big Book" and the *Twelve Steps and Twelve Traditions* do that for us. Rather, this First Step workbook is a guide to an experiential process that allows us to examine our dependencies through a structured format.

As we begin the process of looking hard at the effects that our use of alcohol and/or other drugs have had on our lives, it's important to understand the nature of alcoholism/chemical dependency. The most generally used definition of chemical dependency states that *when the use of alcohol and/or other drugs interferes in any significant area of a person's life and he or she continues to use alcohol and/or drugs in spite of the consequences, that person is an alcoholic or an addict.*

The areas of significance in our lives that are included in this definition involve emotional and spiritual health; physical well-being; relationships with family members and significant others; interaction with society in general; legal concerns; employment; economic/financial aspects. This truth-and-consequences approach avoids our having to deal with issues such as *what* we drink/use, *when* we drink/use, or *how much* we drink/use. It simply focuses on the data which shows exactly how drinking/using has affected our lives. Through this workbook, we can examine our drinking and/or drug use in just this way, by objectively evaluating the impact upon each of these important areas of our lives.

This definition of alcoholism/chemical dependency fits within the framework of the disease concept. Since 1951, alcoholism has been recognized as a disease with predictable stages and symptoms. It is progressive; if untreated, it gets worse. And it is a primary disease; that is, it is not symptomatic of some other disease. The disease of alcoholism/chemical dependency is all-encompassing in its impact; it affects an individual emotionally, socially, intellectually, spiritually, and physically.

Research indicates that most male alcoholics are caught up in a destructive drinking pattern for seven to ten years before they seek help for their problem. For female alcoholics, this period is approximately two to five years. Other chemical dependents experience similar time lags between the onset of dependent use and the subsequent asking for help. This time lag shows that a powerful force exists to prevent alcoholics and other drug dependents from looking for help for their disease. This force is the real cornerstone of any addiction. It is part of the disease yet, ironically, it not only keeps the dependent persons from seeking help, but actually prevents dependents from seeing that they need help.

Delusion and Denial

Any addiction is really a process of delusion and denial. A person is unable to see the onset and progression of his/her alcoholism or drug addiction, and this distorted view allows for the development and progression of the addiction. We can be alcoholic or addicted to other drugs for many years and be basically unaware of our destructive dependencies. This inability to see the reality of our condition leads us to deny its existence. Denial of a condition is not unique to addiction; it can apply to many areas of an individual's life, including other kinds of health issues. What about the overweight person who dresses in navy blue and shuns mirrors in order to shut out reality? Or the heart patient who blames cardiac pain on indigestion? Let's examine some of the ways we build our fortress of denial.

Rationalizing: Rationalizing is a thought process through which we provide a reasonable but untrue reason for consequences resulting from our drinking or other drug use. It is a way of avoiding responsibility for our actions. Rationalizing generates a sincere belief that we are the victims of unique sets of circumstances beyond our control.

For example, I may view my spouse as not providing the kind of support I need. Possibly my spouse's job demands a great deal of time and energy, leaving me responsible for all the decisions involving home and children. I resent what I sense as a lack of emotional support, and I am bored by the daily routine at home, especially when the kids are away at school. Initially, drinking alcohol was a pastime to fill in the lonely, boring hours, but now the drinking has become a problem and has begun to interfere with my marital relationship. This further intensifies the tensions between my spouse and me. I rationalize my drinking by saying I would not drink if my life would change or become more exciting, or if my spouse would be more supportive. Besides, I believe there is nothing wrong with having little pick-me-ups during the day. After all, don't I always get everything done that needs doing?

Through this kind of rationalizing, we provide plausible descriptions of our situations and successfully avoid having to look at the reality of our drinking. It is important to note that rationalizing is an unconscious process and is not deliberate deception.

Projection: Projection means dumping feelings of self-hate onto others; we identify negative characteristics in others that we find distasteful in ourselves.

For instance, I may have an argument with my spouse about my drinking. My response to this argument may be to drive to a nearby bar where I proceed to drink for several hours while lamenting the sorry state of married life. On my way home I am picked up by the police for drunk driving. Instead of dealing with the real issue, the drinking, I focus on my spouse, who "doesn't understand me" and "is always starting arguments," or the police officer who is "angry at the world."

The important point is that, through projection, we don't have to look at our drinking, only the situations or the behavior of others, and therefore we can successfully avoid responsibility for the consequences of our own actions. Projection, like rationalizing, is an unconscious process.

The more we begin to loathe ourselves as our chemical addiction progresses, the more frequently we begin to identify and confront these characteristics in others. Eventually we begin to see ourselves as surrounded by hateful, contemptible, and manipulative people who are interfering with the normal conduct of our lives. Spouses, friends, employers, and others who are close to us become identified in our minds as the cause of our problems or of our drinking and/or other drug use. The more frequently we repeat these "it's all their fault" inner dialogues, the more we distort our views of relationships until we see ourselves as the victims of the actions and attitudes of others.

Repression: Repression is the unconscious blocking of events that are too difficult to deal with. It usually happens when an event or situation generates extremely painful feelings.

For example, a violent, drunken argument with my spouse or significant other has led to physical abuse. Since this action conflicts with my values, I find it too painful to look at. Therefore, I block out the event so that I have absolutely no recollection of it on the following day. Again, this is not a deliberate attempt to distort the truth, but rather an unconscious process that effectively thwarts the ability to recall prior, emotionally painful events.

Other factors, too, are building blocks of denial. One of these is blackouts, chemically induced periods of amnesia. An individual is able to function normally during a blackout, but later has no recollection of what transpired during this period, which may last from a few hours to several days. The experience of a blackout can be extremely frightening and adds to the dependent's increasing sense of confusion.

Another factor is defensiveness. We become defensive whenever any mention is made of a drinking problem. This defensiveness, coupled with a tendency to minimize the extent of our alcohol and drug use, makes us unable to benefit from the input of others and denies us any kind of valid reality testing.

Finally, there are delays; we tend to put off taking any positive action, even when we are aware that we need help, believing that somehow tomorrow will be different. This false expectation of change, in spite of our experience, keeps many of us from reaching out for help.

Although other factors are involved in denial, these are the significant ones. If we pile these together repeatedly over time, they create the phenomenon of denial — the inability to see clearly the reality of our own condition. This workbook is designed to help crumble the walls of denial that have held us captive for so long.

Alcoholics Anonymous says that to begin the journey toward sobriety we must first acknowledge our problem; WE ADMITTED WE WERE POWERLESS OVER ALCOHOL — THAT OUR LIVES HAD BECOME UNMANAGEABLE. Whatever our drug of choice, our admission of powerlessness and unmanageability marks the beginning of recovery.

The Twelve Steps*

1. We admitted we were powerless over alcohol — that our lives had become unmanageable.

2. Came to believe that a Power greater than ourselves could restore us to sanity.

3. Made a decision to turn our will and our lives over to the care of God, as we understood Him.

4. Made a searching and fearless moral inventory of ourselves.

5. Admitted to God, to ourselves and to another human being the exact nature of our wrongs.

6. Were entirely ready to have God remove all these defects of character.

7. Humbly asked Him to remove our shortcomings.

8. Made a list of all persons we had harmed, and became willing to make amends to them all.

9. Made direct amends to such people wherever possible, except when to do so would injure them or others.

10. Continued to take personal inventory and when we were wrong, promptly admitted it.

11. Sought through prayer and meditation to improve our conscious contact with God, as we understood Him, praying only for knowledge of His will for us and the power to carry that out.

12. Having had a spiritual awakening as the result of these steps, we tried to carry this message to alcoholics and to practice these principles in all our affairs.

*The Twelve Steps reprinted by permission of AA World Services, Inc. © 1939, 1955, and 1976.
The interpretations which follow are those of the author, not those of AA, and are neither endorsed nor opposed by AA.

"We admitted we were powerless over alcohol (and/or other drugs) — that our lives had become unmanageable."

You are asked to write a miniature autobiography high-lighting significant events in your life. This tends to put your life in perspective and facilitates working through the First Step. General subject guidelines have been provided in each life stage to assist you in your descriptions. Please feel free to explore beyond the guidelines.

Childhood through preteen years

Quality of relationships with parents and siblings:

_____

_____

_____

_____

_____

_____

_____

_____

_____

_____

Earliest recollections of feelings about myself:

_____

_____

_____

_____

_____

_____

_____

_____

_____

_____

Any significant losses, triumphs, and other experiences:

_____

_____

_____

_____

_____

_____

_____

_____

_____

Religious influences in family life:

_____

_____

_____

_____

_____

_____

_____

_____

_____

_____

Attitudes about male/female roles:

_____

_____

_____

_____

_____

_____

_____

_____

_____

_____

Earliest attitudes about alcoholism/chemical dependency:

_____

_____

_____

_____

_____

_____

_____

_____

_____

Parental use of alcohol and drugs:

_____

_____

_____

_____

_____

_____

_____

_____

_____

Experimentation with or use of alcohol and drugs during this stage:

_____

_____

_____

_____

_____

_____

_____

_____

_____

_____

Teen years

Relationships with parents and siblings during this stage:

_____

_____

_____

_____

_____

_____

_____

_____

_____

_____

Parents' relationship with one another:

_____

_____

_____

_____

_____

_____

_____

_____

_____

Major values that parents attempted to pass on to me:

_____

_____

_____

_____

_____

_____

_____

_____

_____

Attitudes and performance in school:

_____

_____

_____

_____

_____

_____

_____

_____

_____

_____

Involvement in extracurricular activities:

_____

_____

_____

_____

_____

_____

_____

_____

_____

_____

Attitudes about male and female relationships:

_____

_____

_____

_____

_____

_____

_____

_____

_____

_____

Social network during this stage — friends, dating, etc.:

_____

_____

_____

_____

_____

_____

_____

_____

_____

_____

Feelings about myself during this stage:

_____

_____

_____

_____

_____

_____

_____

_____

_____

_____

Any significant losses, successes, or other experiences:

_____

_____

_____

_____

_____

_____

_____

_____

_____

_____

Experimentation with or use of alcohol and other drugs:

_____

_____

_____

_____

_____

_____

_____

_____

_____

_____

Early adult life

Passage into adulthood:

_____

_____

_____

_____

_____

_____

_____

_____

_____

_____

Ongoing relationships with parents and siblings:

_____

_____

_____

_____

_____

_____

_____

_____

_____

_____

Military experience, if any:

_____

_____

_____

_____

_____

_____

_____

_____

_____

Social network at this stage:

_____

_____

_____

_____

_____

_____

_____

_____

_____

The development and outcome of significant relationships, including marriages, separations, and divorces:

_____

_____

_____

_____

_____

_____

_____

_____

_____

_____

Feelings about myself:

_____

_____

_____

_____

_____

_____

_____

_____

_____

_____

Educational and career direction:

_____

_____

_____

_____

_____

_____

_____

_____

_____

_____

Significant losses, successes, other experiences:

_____

_____

_____

_____

_____

_____

_____

_____

_____

_____

Use of alcohol and drugs during this stage:

_____

_____

_____

_____

_____

_____

_____

_____

_____

Effects of drinking/drug use on my life:

_____

_____

_____

_____

_____

_____

_____

_____

_____

Later adult life

Ongoing relationship with family of origin (parents and siblings):

_____

_____

_____

_____

_____

_____

_____

_____

_____

Career success or failure:

_____

_____

_____

_____

_____

_____

_____

_____

_____

Outcome of goals established earlier in life:

_____

_____

_____

_____

_____

_____

_____

_____

_____

Marriage/divorce history; quality of significant
relationships:

_____

_____

_____

_____

_____

_____

_____

_____

_____

Relationships with my children:

_____

_____

_____

_____

_____

_____

_____

_____

_____

Social relationships:

_____

_____

_____

_____

_____

_____

_____

_____

_____

Feelings about myself:

_____

_____

_____

_____

_____

_____

_____

_____

_____

Significant losses, successes, and other experiences:

_____

_____

_____

_____

_____

_____

_____

_____

_____

Drinking and drug use patterns; their impact on my life:

_____

_____

_____

_____

_____

_____

_____

_____

_____

_____

Present

How I view myself:

_____

_____

_____

_____

_____

_____

_____

_____

_____

How I view society and the world I live in:

_____

_____

_____

_____

_____

_____

_____

_____

_____

How I believe other people view me:

_____
_____
_____
_____
_____
_____
_____
_____
_____
_____

How I believe others view my drinking/drug use:

_____
_____
_____
_____
_____
_____
_____
_____
_____
_____

To facilitate working through the First Step, it has been divided into two parts. Part I deals with powerlessness and Part II deals with unmanageability. Powerlessness and unmanageability are related — intertwined, in fact. Unmanageability is the manifestation of powerlessness.

Please respond to the following questions. When you cite an example, try to identify the exact date, time, place, and people involved. The more specific you can be with your responses, the more helpful this process will be for you. Note that examples have been included for clarification purposes only. You do not need to restrict your own examples to those mentioned.

Part I: Powerlessness

1. What does the term "powerlessness" mean to me?

_____

_____

_____

_____

_____

_____

_____

_____

_____

_____

_____

2. How do I see myself as powerless over alcohol and/or other drugs?

_____

_____

_____

_____

_____

_____

_____

_____

_____

_____

_____

3. Progression — Progression involves a change in drinking/drug use over time. This change might involve:
   - Drinking and using greater amounts due to my increased tolerance
   - Drinking and/or using drugs in ways that will get me high more quickly, as in gulping drinks
   - No longer being able to control consistently or predict the outcomes of my drinking/drug use
   - Experiencing a noticeable decrease in my ability to tolerate or handle my drinking/drug use

Three examples of how my drinking and/or drug use has progressed:

_____

_____

_____

_____

_____

_____

_____

_____

_____

_____

_____

_____

_____

_____

_____

_____

_____

_____

4. Attempts at control — How have I previously tried to control my use of alcohol/other drugs? Controlling efforts might have involved:
   - Cutting back on my use
   - Attempts to stop my use
   - Setting time limits ("no drinking before 5:00 p.m.," for instance)
   - Changing drugs or types of alcoholic beverages, as in switching from bourbon to beer

Important note: any attempt to control your drinking and/or drug use is an indication that it is already out of control.

Five examples of how I have attempted to control my drinking/drug use:

_____

_____

_____

_____

_____

_____

_____

_____

_____

_____

_____

_____

_____

_____

_____

_____

_____

_____

_____

_____

_____

_____

_____

_____

5. Preoccupation — How my thinking and activities revolve around my use of alcohol/drugs. This can include:
   - Planning my day around my drinking or drug use
   - Daydreaming about times when I will be free to drink and/or take drugs
   - Structuring my life and activities to create more opportunities/situations for drinking/drug use
   - Compulsively completing tasks to allow time for drinking/using
   - Becoming angry when people or situations interfere with my drinking/using plans

Three examples of preoccupation with my drinking/drug-using:

_____

_____

_____

_____

_____

_____

_____

_____

_____

_____

_____

_____

_____

_____

_____

_____

_____

_____

6. Avoidance/protection — Actions/behaviors I engage in to keep others from being aware of my drinking/drug use. Such behaviors might include:
   - Hiding bottles/drugs
   - Sneaking drinks/drugs
   - Avoiding any reference to my chemical use
   - Frequent use of breath mints or sprays
   - Minimizing amounts of alcohol/drugs consumed
   - Not getting close to others for fear they might smell my breath

Five examples of how I have attempted to keep others from knowing about my drinking/drug use:

_____

_____

_____

_____

_____

_____

_____

_____

_____

_____

_____

_____

_____

_____

_____

_____

_____

_____

_____

_____

_____

_____

_____

_____

_____

7. Loss of control — The inability to predict the outcome or consequences of my drinking/drug use. This might include:
   - Being unable to quit once I start drinking/using
   - Attempting to quit drinking/using "for good" but being unable to succeed
   - Drinking or using more than I'd intended
   - Being unable to keep social, family, business engagements because of my drinking/using
   - Behaving when I have been drinking/using in ways that conflict with my values (doing something while under the influence that I would not normally do)
   - Getting myself into embarrassing or dangerous situations
   - Being arrested for actions related to my drinking/using (as in a drunk driving charge)

Five examples of loss of control related to my drinking/ using:

_____

_____

_____

_____

_____

_____

_____

_____

_____

_____

_____

_____

_____

_____

_____

_____

_____

_____

_____

_____

_____

_____

_____

_____

_____

_____

8. Destructive/dangerous behavior — Engaging in
    destructive, aggressive, or dangerous behavior while
    drinking/using drugs. This can include:
    - Being verbally or physically abusive to others
    - Engaging in self-destructive behavior, such as drink-
      ing when my doctor has advised against it
    - Driving my car with my children as passengers
      while under the influence
    - Being unable to provide adequately for my chil-
      dren's physical or safety needs while under the
      influence
    - Contemplating or attempting suicide
    - Threatening others with guns, knives, or other
      lethal instruments
    - Driving or operating dangerous equipment or
      machinery while under the influence
    - Mixing drugs and alcohol, even though I know the
      danger involved

Three examples of destructive/dangerous behaviors:

_____

_____

_____

_____

_____

_____

_____

_____

_____

_____

_____

_____

_____

_____

_____

_____

_____

_____

9. Justifying drinking/using — Ways in which I have shifted the responsibility for drinking/using onto someone or something else. Justifying behavior can include:
   - Pointing to people or situations as the cause of my drinking/using problem (blaming my spouse or my parents, or the fact that I'm currently out of a job and had an argument with my girlfriend)
   - Blaming an emotional state ("I'm depressed," or "I feel nervous and uptight," or "I'm under a lot of pressure at work")
   - Saying "Everyone does it" or "It's no one's business what I do to myself"

Five examples of how I have not taken responsibility for my drinking/drug use:

_____

_____

_____

_____

_____

_____

_____

_____

_____

_____

_____

_____

_____

_____

_____

_____

_____

_____

_____

_____

_____

_____

_____

_____

10. Differences in perception — Alcohol is a deluding drug, as are all mood-altering substances. They distort our perceptions of real world events so that our recollections of drinking/using episodes may conflict with the recollections of others. Perceptual differences might involve:
    - Being told that I was verbally abusive at a party when my recollection is that I was charming and entertaining
    - Believing that I was sober and in control at a certain event, only to be advised by my family that I was drunk and staggering
    - Having people share their concerns with me about my drinking/drug use when I did not see it as a problem

Three examples of drinking/using situations in which I was confronted with evidence from family/friends/co-workers that contradicted my own recollections of events and behaviors:

_____

_____

_____

_____

_____

11. *This is the end of Part I on powerlessness. Review your responses to the questions on powerlessness and note the five most important examples that support the fact that you are powerless over alcohol/drugs and why are they significant to you.*

_____

_____

_____

_____

_____

_____

_____

_____

_____

_____

_____

_____

_____

_____

_____

_____

_____

_____

_____

_____

12. *Refer to pages 29 and 30 and review your answers to questions 1 and 2. Now that you have completed this section, briefly indicate what you have learned about your powerlessness over alcohol/drugs.*

_____

_____

_____

_____

_____

_____

_____

_____

_____

_____

_____

_____

_____

_____

_____

_____

_____

_____

_____

Part II: Unmanageability

1. What does unmanageability mean to me?

_____

_____

_____

_____

_____

_____

_____

_____

_____

_____

2. How do I see my life as unmanageable as a result of alcohol/drug use?

_____

_____

_____

_____

_____

_____

_____

_____

_____

_____

_____

_____

3. Social life — How drinking/drug use has affected my
   social life:
   - Do I associate primarily with people who drink
     and use?
   - Do I find myself avoiding non-drinking/using
     friends and situations?
   - Do family members or friends try to keep me from
     drinking situations?
   - Do I find that I am becoming more socially
     isolated, preferring to do my drinking/using in
     private to avoid being interrupted?

Three examples of how my social life has been affected by
my drinking/drug use:

_____

_____

_____

_____

_____

_____

_____

_____

_____

_____

_____

_____

_____

_____

_____

_____

_____

4. Physical condition — What impact has my drinking had on me physically? How has it affected my general health?
   - Do I have difficulty sleeping?
   - Do I frequently use antacids for stomach distress?
   - Do I find myself without energy?
   - Do I suffer from frequent diarrhea?
   - Have I experienced a general deterioration in body tone and physical appearance?
   - Have I gained or lost weight?
   - Do I continue to drink/use in spite of my doctor's recommendation to stop?
   - Do I withhold my real drinking/using history from my doctor?

Three examples of how drinking/drug use has affected me physically:

_____

_____

_____

_____

_____

_____

_____

_____

_____

_____

_____

_____

_____

_____

_____

_____

5. Economic impact — What effect has drinking/drug use had on my financial condition? This might involve:
   - Poor investment decisions
   - Overspending; piling up debts
   - Mismanagement of household funds
   - Lack of savings
   - Lack of adequate financial preparation for retirement
   - Allowing alcohol/drug purchases to take precedence over domestic needs
   - Loss of job promotions and/or loss of jobs

Three examples of how drinking/drug use has affected me economically:

_____

_____

_____

_____

_____

_____

_____

_____

_____

_____

_____

Direct cost estimates — direct costs for alcohol/drug purchases

daily: $_____

weekly: $_____

monthly: $_____

annually: $_____

Indirect cost estimates — the dollar impact of legal fees, court costs, fines, lost job promotions/jobs, poor investment decisions, etc., related to drinking/drug use

$_____

How do my drinking or drug-related costs compare with costs for essentials (food, housing, etc.)?

_____

_____

_____

Approximately what percentage of my income is spent on my alcohol/drug use or related costs?

$_____

6. *The following questions pertain to what you do in your job, at school, at home, or in retirement. Complete the categories that currently apply or have applied in the past. For example, if you are currently employed but also had problems with alcohol and/or drugs while going to school, examine the impact in both categories.*

In my job/profession — What impact has my drinking/drug use had on my work/career? Problems can surface in areas such as:
- Lowered productivity
- Deteriorating quality of product or decision-making
- Being passed up for promotion
- Being terminated from a position even though my drinking/drug use might not have been mentioned as a reason
- Frequent absenteeism
- Conflicts with peers/subordinates/superiors
- Being placed on disciplinary probation
- Being forced into early retirement
- Feeling guilty about quality/quantity of job performance even though it has never been questioned
- Being confronted by colleagues or co-workers about my alcohol/drug use

Three examples of how my drinking/drug use has created problems in my job or profession:

_____

_____

_____

_____

_____

_____

_____

_____

_____

_____

_____

_____

_____

_____

_____

_____

At home — If I am partly or totally responsible for managing a household, problems like these may surface:
- Being unable to accomplish daily chores
- Compulsively finishing household tasks so I will be free to drink and/or use drugs
- Being unable to provide adequately for my children's emotional, physical, or safety needs while under the influence (transporting children after drinking, for instance, or not providing adequate or on-time meals)
- Engaging in conflicts with children/other family members/significant other over alcohol/drug use
- Engaging in conflicts over shared household responsibilities
- Hiding supply or amount consumed from other family members
- Cutting off drinking before children or spouse gets home
- Losing interest in activities or hobbies
- Getting into embarrassing situations with family or family friends
- Having difficulty keeping appointments/commitments

Three examples of how my drinking/drug use has interfered with household or parental responsibilities:

_____

_____

_____

_____

_____

_____

_____

_____

_____

_____

_____

_____

_____

_____

_____

_____

_____

In school — If I am a student, problems like these may surface:

- Not keeping up with homework assignments
- Frequent absenteeism
- Dropping classes or dropping out of school
- Being involved in a disciplinary action, such as suspension
- Lower grades or a drop in grade average
- Bringing alcohol/drugs to school
- Associating primarily with other students who are using alcohol and drugs
- Dropping out of or not participating in extracurricular activities

Three examples of how my drinking/drug use has inter-fered with social activities or education:

_____

_____

_____

_____

_____

_____

_____

_____

_____

_____

_____

_____

_____

_____

_____

_____

_____

_____

Retirement — If I am retired, problems like these may arise:

- Retiring before I was financially prepared to do so
- Being unable to act on prior retirement plans/dreams
- Losing interest in hobbies or activities
- Becoming more socially isolated
- Finding that fixed income doesn't cover expenses because of the cost of alcohol/drugs
- Engaging in more frequent conflicts with my spouse over my drinking/drug use
- Spending a great deal of time focusing on the past

Three examples of how my drinking/drug use has affected my retirement:

_____

_____

_____

_____

_____

_____

_____

_____

_____

_____

_____

_____

_____

_____

_____

_____

_____

_____

7. Value conflicts — Behaving while drinking/using drugs in ways that conflict with my values or beliefs. This might include:
   - Theft of money or goods to support my drinking/drug use
   - Passing bad checks
   - Padding my expense accounts
   - Becoming involved in sexual relationships outside of marriage or relationship with a significant other
   - Becoming hostile or violent
   - Physically or emotionally abusing family members or friends
   - Losing interest in my appearance/personal hygiene
   - Depriving family of my love and emotional support
   - Lying to family/friends/employers
   - Contemplating or attempting suicide
   - Turning my back on my religious or spiritual beliefs

_____

_____

_____

_____

_____

8. Spiritual problems — How has drinking/drug use affected me spiritually? This can include:
   - Having vague spiritual desires but no spiritual direction
   - A sense that life has no meaning
   - A feeling of emptiness
   - Moving from belief to agnosticism/atheism as my addiction progresses
   - Becoming upset at or hostile towards any reference to religion or religious beliefs
   - Staying away from church because of guilt feelings

Three examples of how my drinking/drug use has affected me spiritually:

_____

_____

_____

_____

_____

_____

9. Emotional problems — How has drinking/drug use affected me emotionally? Emotional problems can include:
   - Depression
   - Feeling that I am going crazy
   - Feeling that others are against me
   - Feelings of low self-esteem
   - Fear of social situations
   - Lack of intimacy; difficulty in getting close to others or in expressing feelings
   - Being very intolerant or rigid in my thinking and in relationships with others
   - Feelings of rage
   - Angry outbursts or temper tantrums
   - Feelings of panic when drinking/using plans are changed or cancelled
   - Unexplained fears
   - Extreme feelings of loneliness
   - Overwhelming guilt feelings
   - Sense of impending doom
   - Vivid nightmares
   - Contemplated or attempted suicide
   - Rapid mood swings from euphoria to depression

Five examples of how my drinking/drug use has affected me emotionally:

_____

_____

_____

_____

_____

10. Sexual problems — How has drinking/drug use affected me sexually? Sexual problems can involve:
- Difficulty in achieving or maintaining erection
- Inability to achieve orgasm
- Loss of interest in sex generally
- Interest in sex only when drinking/using
- Partner has lost interest in sex
- While drinking/using, becoming involved in sexual relationships outside of marriage or relationship with a significant other
- Sexual identity conflicts as the result of sexual experiences — while drinking/using — with someone of a different sex than is my usual preference
- Becoming sexually promiscuous
- Having sexual problems as an identified homosexual, or if I am a homosexual who has chosen to keep my sexual preference a private matter, violating — while drinking/using — my own commitment to privacy

Five examples of how my drinking/drug use has affected me sexually:

_____

_____

_____

_____

_____

11. Life goal problems — How has drinking/drug use kept me from accomplishing my goals? Life goal problems can involve:
- Education issues, such as failure to complete classes, terms, or degree programs
- Being unprepared or unable to enter desired career/profession
- Inability to grow within current career field
- Inability to develop family/marital relationships according to my expectations
- Inability to find spouse or significant other to share my life
- Inability to put plans or ideas into action
- Frequent goal-changing; scattered aims
- General lack of career motivation

Three examples of how my drinking/drug use has kept me from accomplishing my goals:

_____

_____

_____

_____

_____

_____

_____

_____

_____

_____

_____

_____

_____

_____

_____

_____

_____

12. Family problems — How has drinking/drug use interfered with relationships that mean the most to me? Family problems can involve:
- Verbal abuse
- Emotional abuse
- Physical abuse
- Loss of closeness
- A feeling that other family members have lost respect for me.
- A sense of no longer being part of family
- Using family members emotionally, financially
- Feeling out of control as a parent, as children act out sexually, become involved with alcohol/drugs, withdraw, have school problems, refuse to talk to me
- Making sexual advances to or becoming sexually involved with my child/children
- Feeling depressed, angry, or justified because my spouse is now drinking/using as I do
- Extreme feelings of guilt and remorse
- Feeling lonely ("no one understands me")
- Withdrawing from family activities
- Separation from spouse and children
- Divorce

Three examples for each family member: how my drinking/drug use has affected each individual and the quality of my relationship with him or her:

Spouse or significant other — Three examples of how my drinking/drug use has affected . . .

_____
(name)

_____

_____

_____

_____

_____

_____

_____

_____

_____

_____

_____

_____

_____

_____

_____

_____

_____

_____

First child — Three examples of how my drinking/
drug use has affected . . .

(name)	(age)

_____

_____

_____

_____

_____

_____

_____

_____

_____

_____

_____

_____

_____

_____

_____

Second child — Three examples of how my drinking/ drug use has affected . . .

_____
(name)   (age)

_____

_____

_____

_____

_____

_____

_____

_____

_____

_____

_____

_____

_____

_____

_____

Third child — Three examples of how my drinking/
drug use has affected . . .

_____
(name)   (age)

_____

_____

_____

_____

_____

_____

_____

_____

_____

_____

_____

_____

_____

_____

_____

_____

_____

_____

_____

Fourth child — Three examples of how my drinking/
drug use has affected . . .

_____
            (name)   (age)

_____

_____

_____

_____

_____

_____

_____

_____

_____

_____

_____

_____

_____

_____

_____

_____

_____

_____

*Note: If more children are involved whether by current or
previous relationships, including stepchildren, use a sepa-
rate sheet of paper.*

Mother — Three examples of how my drinking/drug use has affected my mother:

_____

_____

_____

_____

_____

_____

_____

_____

_____

_____

_____

_____

_____

_____

_____

_____

_____

Father — Three examples of how my drinking/drug use has affected my father:

_____

_____

_____

_____

_____

_____

_____

_____

_____

_____

_____

_____

_____

_____

_____

_____

_____

_____

(name of brother or sister)

Friends — Three examples of how my drinking/drug use has affected my friends:

_____
(friend's name)

_____

_____

_____

_____

_____

_____

_____

_____

_____

_____

_____

_____

_____

_____

_____

_____

_____

_____

(friend's name)

_____

_____

_____

_____

_____

_____

_____

_____

_____

_____

_____

_____

_____

_____

_____

_____

_____

(friend's name)

(friend's name)

13. *Review your responses to the questions pertaining to family and friends beginning on page 67. Briefly indicate what you have learned about the impact your drinking and/or drug use has had upon your family and friends.*

_____

_____

_____

_____

_____

_____

_____

_____

_____

_____

_____

_____

_____

_____

_____

_____

_____

_____

_____

_____

_____

14. *This is the end of Part II on unmanageability. Review your responses to the questions on unmanageability beginning on page 45 and note the eight most significant examples that support the fact that your life is unmanageable as a result of your alcohol/drug use.*

15. *Refer to page 45 and review your answers to questions 1 and 2. Now that you have completed this section, indicate briefly what you have learned about how your life has been and is unmanageable as a result of your alcohol/drug use.*

_____

_____

_____

_____

_____

_____

_____

_____

_____

_____

_____

_____

_____

_____

_____

_____

_____

_____

_____

In summary

1. *Now that you have completed this First Step work-book, describe in narrative form what you have learned from this process. Do you see yourself as being chemically dependent or not? Explain your answer.*

2. *If your answer is yes, go on to number 3. If your answer is no, you need to reevaluate your First Step. If you are presently in a chemical dependency program and have been asked to complete this workbook as part of your therapy, chances are good that alcohol/ drugs are a problem for you. If you are not in treatment, the fact that you are working this Step is evidence of concern about your use of chemicals. In either case, you need to follow up this Step by asking others to validate or repudiate your objectivity in perceiving the reality of your situation. Remember, one of the most important symptoms of addiction is the addict's inability to see the reality of his or her condition.*

3. *If after reviewing the First Step you determine that you are alcoholic/chemically dependent, give five reasons why you need ongoing help and support for your problem.*

_____

_____

_____

_____

_____

Our admission of powerlessness and unmanageability marks the beginning of recovery. But we must go beyond admission to acceptance — acceptance of our dependency and the realization that we need ongoing help to achieve comfortable sobriety.

Help is available in many forms. Chemical dependency treatment centers offer successful programs in learning to live free of alcohol and other drugs. Medical and mental health professionals who specialize in working with the chemically dependent can be of valuable assistance. And the Twelve Step Program of Alcoholics Anonymous (AA) offers the most effective tools for recovery available.

Completing this workbook for a good First Step has brought us insights and data from our own lives; we will refer to these many times during our recovery. For the Twelve Steps are not a once-and-for-all Program, but a continuing process of growth. Reviewing this completed First Step effort periodically sharpens our awareness of how drugs and alcohol took control of our lives and made them unmanageable, and reinforces our commitment to live sober and straight.

About the author

Richard A. Hamel's *A Good First Step* grew out of his wide experience as an addictions counselor. He has been involved in the field of addiction and recovery since 1970 — since 1976 specifically in the treatment area as a counselor and counselor trainer. He is currently an alcoholism therapist at Westcenter Alcoholism Unit, Tucson General Hospital in Arizona.

He earned an undergraduate degree in business administration from Golden Gate University, San Francisco, and a master's degree in addiction studies from University of Arizona. He has participated in workshops and programs on addictions in many parts of the country, including Minneapolis, where he took part in a Johnson Institute seminar and in St. Mary's Hospital family program.

He and his wife and two children live in Tucson.

Excerpt from the 12-step classic *A Day at a Time*

OCTOBER 3 Reflection for the Day

I've learned in The Program that I'm wholly power-less over my addiction. At long last, I've conceded my powerlessness; as a result, my life has taken a 180-degree turn for the better. However, I *do* have a power, derived from God, to change my own life. I've learned that *acceptance* does not mean *submission* to an unpleasant or degrading situation. It means accepting the reality of the situation and then deciding what, if anything, I can and will do about it. *Have I stopped trying to control the uncontrollable? Am I gaining the courage to change the things I can?*

Today I Pray

I ask my Higher Power for direction as I learn to sort out the things I can change from the things I can't, for that sorting process does, indeed, require God-given wisdom. May "the things I cannot change" not give me an excuse for inaction. May "the things I can" not include managing other people's lives. May I start to understand my own reality.

Today I Will Remember

Acceptance is not inaction. Change is not domination.

A Day at a Time

Deluxe gift edition	$10.95
Paperback edition	$7.95
Classic hardcover	$8.95

Get your copy of *A Day at a Time* at your local bookstore, by using the order form on the next page, or by calling CompCare Publishers toll free at 1-800-328-3330.

Order Form

Order No.	Qty.	Title	Author	Unit Cost	Total
126-9		A Day at a Time—Audio		$9.95	
001-7		—Deluxe Gift		$10.95	
196-X		—Paperback		$7.95	
000-9		—Classic Rust		$8.95	
262-1		Daddy, Please Say You're Sorry	Amber	$12.95	
064-5		Do I Have to Give Up Me to			
		Be Loved by You?	Drs. Paul	$12.95	
269-9		Out of the Shadows	Dr. Patrick Carnes	$11.95	
290-7		A Gentle Path through the Twelve Steps	Dr. Patrick Carnes	$14.95	
				Subtotal	
				Shipping and Handling (see below)	
				Add your state's sales tax	
				TOTAL	

Send check or money order payable to CompCare Publishers. No cash or C.O.D.s please. Quantity discounts available. Prices subject to change without notice.

SHIPPING/HANDLING CHARGES

Order Amount	Shipping Charges
$0.00 - $10.00	$3.50
$10.01 - $25.00	$4.00
$25.01 - $50.00	$5.00
$50.01 - $75.00	$7.00

Send book(s) to:

Name _____

Address _____

City_____State_____Zip_____

❑ Check enclosed for $_____, payable to CompCare Publishers

❑ Charge my credit card   ❑ Visa   ❑ MasterCard   ❑ Discover

Account #_____Exp. Date _____

Signature_____Daytime Phone _____

CompCare® Publishers
3850 Annapolis Lane, Suite 100 • Minneapolis, MN 55447-5443
(612) 559-4800 or toll free (800) 328-3330